Battlelines

Battlelines

World War I
Posters from the
Bowman Gray
Collection

Libby Chenault

Foreword by Arthur S. Link

The Rare Book Collection
Wilson Library
The University of North Carolina
at Chapel Hill

©1988 Rare Book Collection,

Wilson Library,

University of North Carolina at Chapel Hill

Manufactured in the United States of America

Library of Congress Cataloging-in-Publication Data

University of North Carolina at Chapel Hill. Rare
   Book Collection.
   Battlelines: World War I posters from the Bowman Gray
collection.

   Bibliography: p.
   1. World War, 1914–1918—Posters—Private collections—
North Carolina—Chapel Hill—Catalogs. 2. Gray, Bowman—
Poster collections—Catalogs. 3. University of North Carolina
at Chapel Hill. Rare Book Collection—Catalogs. I. Chenault,
Libby. II. Title. III. Title: Battle lines. IV. Bowman Gray collection.
D522.25.U55   1988   940.3'022'Z   87-72897
   ISBN 0-8078-4215-X (pbk.: alk. paper)

Distributed for the Rare Book Collection

by the University of North Carolina Press,

Chapel Hill and London

Contents

Foreword

The period of World War I marks a high point in the history of the graphic arts, particularly cartoons and posters. A casual examination of this book—a selection of the best war posters from around the world—makes this fact evident. But this collection also demonstrates that art and history intersected in a remarkable way from 1914 to 1918, as the great cartoonists, including James Montgomery Flagg, Charles Dana Gibson, and Howard Chandler Christy, to mention only three Americans, turned art to the service of war.

Posters were the belligerents' prime means of propaganda and recruitment; their most effective way of gaining popular support for war loans, conservation of food and fuel, Belgian relief, succor of the wounded, and support for the men in the trenches; and their primary vehicle for making appeals to women and children. Thus one can see in graphic form much of the military and social history of the wartime period. These posters are redolent of the grand clash of arms that rocked the world during four awful years.

This book includes posters from all the major belligerents, but it focuses on those from Great Britain, France, Germany, and the United States. What strikes one most about the posters is the way that graphic artists so well conveyed intimations of the souls and spirits of their own nations. The German posters try to reflect the might and power of German arms. They are heroic and blunt. The British posters reflect the "Bulldog" spirit of a tenacious determination to see the war through to victory. The French posters are more artistic and poignant in their depiction of the human toll of war, a feature totally absent from the German posters. In stark contrast is the optimism, almost exuberance, of the American posters, with their appeals to a nation to rise in arms to save liberty and civilization.

Another striking feature of these posters is the relative absence of appeals to hatred and passion and of the highlighting of alleged atrocities by the enemy. It was as if all the warring peoples shared not only a common concern for country but also an understanding of their common encounter with tragedy.

Libby Chenault has performed a notable service in selecting and arranging the posters reproduced in this book. Still more important is her catalogue of artists. It is a scholarly achievement of the first order.

Arthur S. Link
George Henry Davis '86 Professor
  of American History and
Director and Editor of
  The Papers of Woodrow Wilson

Princeton, New Jersey
November 5, 1987

Acknowledgment

The University acknowledges its debt to the
Gray family for providing the core collection,
and for the support that has allowed this
valuable collection to be made accessible.

This catalogue is dedicated to the memory of
Bowman Gray III.

Battlelines

The Bowman Gray Collection of World Wars I and II

This catalogue marks the completion of a four-year project to provide complete, on-line access to the graphic portion of the Bowman Gray Collection of World Wars I and II.

Bowman Gray first presented war materials to the University of North Carolina Library in 1942. The Gray family continued to expand the collection with gifts in 1946, 1947, and 1950. The focus of this catalogue is the World War I posters, which represent only a fraction of the more than 16,000 graphic items—including an estimated 4,100 posters, 2,400 World War I broadsides, 3,000 photographs, 4,700 postcards, 800 portraits and battle scenes, and over 1,000 miscellaneous items such as original drawings, maps, and leaflets. In addition to the graphic materials, the Gray Collection includes historic documents, books, pamphlets, and serial publications that are part of the University Library collection.

The graphic materials in the Gray Collection received relatively little attention from the Library in the years following the initial gift. Limited exhibitions of the posters were held in Wilson Library in 1946 and 1950, and at the Ackland Art Museum in 1969 (at the time of the Ackland exhibit, a catalogue, *World War Propaganda Posters*, was produced). In 1982, the Gray family provided funds to the Rare Book Collection so that a librarian could be hired for the cataloguing project. Over the next four years, the graphic materials were arranged and catalogued. Additional gifts expanded the collection, and records for all items became part of the local and OCLC data bases.

Continued work on the collection is planned. At this time, the graphic materials are available in the Rare Book Collection for study and publication. A few of the ways in which the Gray images have been used over the last four years are: as visual aids for classes and lectures, in university publications, and for a public television documentary on Woodrow Wilson.

War Posters

It is now more than seventy years since the First World War began, and to many it seems as distant as the Civil War, the Napoleonic Wars, or perhaps even the Punic Wars.

The First World War has been called the first modern war because of the "advances" in warfare on the battlefield. It may also be viewed as "modern" in its introduction of a powerful propaganda weapon, the war poster.

Posters were not the unique creation of any warring government. The first colored posters appeared in the 1860s and the ensuing years saw the development of more sophisticated printing presses and lithographic methods. By 1914 the poster was an accepted advertising medium and art posters were being collected abroad, and so it happened that the First World War coincided with an apex in the development of the poster.

The publicity aspect of the war poster had its origin in the broadside, a posted, official announcement. War posters were also official in nature but differed from broadsides in the prominence of their visual appeal. There was text as well as a visual image, but captions were short—posters were not meant to be studied but rather to produce an immediate and, one would hope, lasting emotional response.

The prominence and widespread use of the poster as a propaganda tool in the First World War has never been equaled. War posters were used by countries on both sides of the conflict and, as holdings from some sixteen countries suggest, by both large countries and small.

The war poster was exploited by warring governments to solicit recruits, to secure war loans, to urge conservation, and to announce and make acceptable national policies. The poster was also used widely by charitable and civic groups. For charitable organizations such as the Red Cross, the YMCA, the RSPCA, and relief groups, the poster made appeals for volunteers, donations, civilian relief, and universal compassion. For civic groups, the poster announced programs, broadcasted appeals, and urged emotional involvement in the war or related causes.

Lefler, Heinrich
1863–1919
ZEICHNET 4.
KRIEGSANLEIHE.
(Subscribe to the 4th
War Loan.)
Austria 1917.
126 × 95 cm.

6

Neumont, Maurice
1868–1930
ON NE PASSE PAS!
(They Shall Not Pass!)
France 1918.
113 × 80 cm.

Weigand, E.

DEUTSCHES HILFSWERK
FÜR KRIEGS- UND
ZIVILGEFANGENEN. GEBE
JEDER SIE LEIDEN FÜR
UNS! IHR LOS ZU
VERBESSERN, IST
EHRENPFLICHT. . . .
(German Assistance
for Military and
Civilian Prisoners.
Everyone Give, They
Suffer for Us! Your
Duty Is to Improve
Their Plight. . . .)
Germany 1914–1918.
142 × 94 cm.

Biro, Mihaly
1886–1949
UNGARISCHES ROTHES-
KREUZ-LOS. . . .
(Hungarian Red Cross
Lottery. . . .)
Hungary 1914–1918.
126 × 94 cm.

**Mauzan, Luciano
Achille**
1883–

PRESTITO DELLA
LIBERAZIONE.

(Liberation Loan.)

Italy 1914–1918.

142 × 102 cm.

Cheptŝov, E.

PODPISYVAĬTES′NA
VOENNYĬ 5½% ZAEM—
CHĨEM BOL′ SHE DENEG,
TĨEM BOL′ SHE
SNARĨADNOV!

(Subscribe to the
5½% War Loan—
the More Money,
the More Missiles!)
Russia 1914–1917.
107 × 72 cm.

Spear, Fred

ENLIST.

United States [1915].

83 × 59 cm.

Appeals

Griessler, Franz

MARINE-SCHAUSPIEL
IN DER
KRIEGSAUSSTELLUNG.
VOLLSTÄNDIG NEUES
PROGRAMM. TÄGLICH
AB 5 UHR
VORSTELLUNGEN....
(Navy Exhibition in
the War Exhibition.
Entirely New
Program. Daily
Presentation from 5
O'Clock....)
Austria 1914–1918.
95 × 63 cm.

McNeill, J.

OUR DUMB FRIENDS'
LEAGUE (A SOCIETY FOR
THE ENCOURAGEMENT
OF KINDNESS TO
ANIMALS) . . . BLUE
CROSS FUND. . . .

England [1917].
77 × 51 cm.

RUSSIA'S DAY, NOV. 18TH.
ORGANISATION OFFICES
5, ARGYLL PLACE,
LONDON, W.

England 1914–1918.
77 × 51 cm.

Buchel, Charles A.
BELGIAN RED CROSS.
England 1914–1918.
77 × 51 cm with
14 × 46 cm sheet
attached to recto.

18

Pegram, Frederick
1870–1937

SEND THEM ALL
SNAP-SHOTS FROM
HOME! Y.M.C.A.

England 1914–1918.
51 × 77 cm.

Thomas, Bert

1883–1966

"THUMBS UP" PATRON
OF THE FUND QUEEN
ALEXANDRA.
WOUNDED SOLDIERS
AND SAILORS "FAG" DAY.
TUESDAY. MAY 29TH
1917. THE SMOKE FUND
OFFICIALLY APPROVED
BY THE WAR OFFICE &
ADMIRALTY. OFFICES:—
4 BUCKINGHAM GATE,
S.W.

England 1917.
77 × 51 cm.

20

STAR & GARTER HOME
for
TOTALLY DISABLED SOLDIERS AND SAILORS
PATRONS: H.M. THE QUEEN & H.M. QUEEN ALEXANDRA

Haven

You can never repay these utterly broken men. But you can show your gratitude by helping to build this Home where they will be tenderly cared for during the rest of their lives.
LET EVERY WOMAN SEND WHAT SHE CAN TO-DAY
to the Lady Cowdray, Hon. Treasurer, The British Women's Hospital Fund, 21 Old Bond Street, W

Special Reproductions of the Cartoon, suitable for framing, can be obtained at above address

Partridge, J.
Bernard, Sir
1861–1945
STAR & GARTER HOME
FOR TOTALLY DISABLED
SOLDIERS AND
SAILORS....
England 1914–1918.
77 × 51 cm.

Praill, R. G.

ENLISTED FOR
DURATION OF THE WAR.
HELP THE NATIONAL
EGG COLLECTION FOR
THE WOUNDED. 154
FLEET ST. LONDON E.C.

England 1914–1918.
77 × 51 cm.

Gawthorn, H. G.

"TUBS FOR TOMMIES."
£10 WILL PROVIDE A
UNIT OF 4 BATHS, WITH
STOVE, BOILER, TOWELS,
SOAP, SCRUBBERS AND
ALL EQUIPMENT....

England 1914–1918.
77 X 51 cm.

OUR CHILDREN'S DAY . . .
OCTOBER 8TH. PLEASE
HELP TO FEED AND
CLOTHE THE 5000
CHILDREN NOW UNDER
THE CARE OF THE WAIFS
& STRAYS SOCIETY. . . .
England 1914–1918.
77 × 51 cm.

Scott, Septimus Edwin

NATIONAL BABY WEEK, 1ST–7TH JULY. "SAVE THE BABIES."

England [1917].

77 × 51 cm.

LE CARDINAL MERCIER PROTÈGE LA BELGIQUE

Fouqueray, Dominique Charles
1872–1956

LE CARDINAL MERCIER PROTÉGE LA BELGIQUE.

(Cardinal Mercier Protects Belgium.)

France [1916].
120 × 81 cm.

Cattier, Raymond

ŒUVRE DES MASSEURS
AVEUGLES DE LA
GUERRE. DONNEZ POUR
EUX MÊME LA PLUS
PETITE OFFRANDE. . . .

(Work of the Masseurs
Blinded in the War.
Give Them at Least
the Smallest of
Offerings. . . .)

France 1918.
80 × 120 cm.

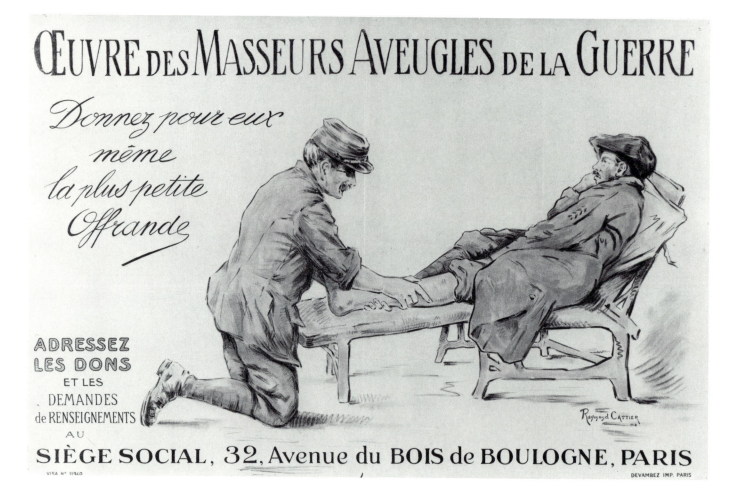

SALLE DU TROCADÉRO
JEUDI 24 FÉVRIER 1916 A 2 H½ PRÉCISES

GRANDE MATINÉE ARTISTIQUE
EN L'HONNEUR DE RAEMAEKERS
AU PROFIT DES ŒUVRES DE GUERRE FRANCO-HOLLANDAISES
ORGANISÉE SUR L'INITIATIVE DU RAPPEL ET SOUS LE PATRONAGE DES PRÉSIDENTS
DU SÉNAT, DE LA CHAMBRE, DU CONSEIL DES MINISTRES ET DU CONSEIL MUNICIPAL

PROJECTIONS DES ŒUVRES DE RAEMAEKERS
COMMENTÉES PAR MM. GRAND-CARTERET ET FUNCK-BRENTANO

PARTIE DE CONCERT AVEC LE CONCOURS DE
Mᴸˡᴱˢ BOURDON ET BUGG (DE L'OPÉRA), Mᴸˡᴱˢ CHASLES ET BOS (DE L'OPÉRA)
Mᴸˡᴱˢ MARIE LECONTE ET MORENO (DE LA COMÉDIE FRANÇAISE), Mᴸˡᴱ O'BRIEN (DE L'OPÉRA-COMIQUE)
Mᴸˡᴱ MARTHA DE VILLERS, DE M. XAVIER LEROUX ET DES ARTISTES HOLLANDAIS
MM. HOLLMAN, H. ALBERS, J. REDER, DAVID BLITZ
ET DE LA MUSIQUE DE LA GARDE RÉPUBLICAINE
REFRAINS ET SONNERIES DE L'ARMÉE FRANÇAISE

PRIX DES PLACES : LOGES A 500ᶠ ET 200ᶠ DONNANT DROIT A DES ŒUVRES D'ART
ORCHESTRE 5ᶠ - LOGES 4ᶠ - BALCON 3ᶠ - AMPHITHÉÂTRE 2ᶠ - TRIBUNES 1ᶠ
ON PEUT LOUER SANS AUGMENTATION DE PRIX AU TROCADÉRO - A L'AGENCE DES THÉÂTRES, 38, AVENUE DE L'OPÉRA
CHEZ DURAND, 6, PLACE DE LA MADELEINE, ET AUX AMIS DE PARIS, 167, RUE MONTMARTRE
Imp. H. CHACHOIN, PARIS (Atelier Maurice NEUMONT, 1, Place du Calvaire)

Neumont, Maurice
1868–1930

SALLE DU TROCADÉRO.
JEUDI 24 FÉVRIER 1916 A
2H ½ PRÉCISES. GRANDE
MATINÉE ARTISTIQUE
EN L'HONNEUR DE
RAEMAEKERS AU PROFIT
DES ŒUVRES DE GUERRE
FRANCO-
HOLLANDAISES. . . .

(Salle du Trocadéro.
Thursday, 24 February
1916, at Exactly 2:30.
Grande Matinée
Artistique in Honor of
Raemaekers for the
Benefit of the Franco-
Dutch War Work. . . .)
France 1916.
119 × 89 cm.

Steinlen, Théophile Alexandre
1859–1923

EN BELGIQUE LES BELGES ONT FAIM. TOMBOLA ARTISTIQUE AU PROFIT DE L'ALIMENTATION POPULAIRE DE BELGIQUE—CHAQUE BILLET DE CINQ FRANCS DONNE DROIT....

(In Belgium the Belgians Are Hungry. Tombola Artistique for the Benefit of the Alimentation Populaire of Belgium. Each Five-Franc Ticket Gives the Right....)
France 1915.
130 × 94 cm.

EN BELGIQUE LES BELGES ONT FAIM

TOMBOLA ARTISTIQUE au profit de L'ALIMENTATION POPULAIRE DE BELGIQUE__ CHAQUE BILLET DE CINQ FRANCS DONNE DROIT:

A__ à un souvenir, œuvre spéciale: soit une gravure du peintre FIRMIN BAES__ soit une médaille breloque du sculpteur DEVREESE,

B__ au tirage de la tombola des dons d'ART APPLIQUÉ__ (DENTELLES, BRODERIES,__ PEINTURES SUR VASES,__ SOIERIES, etc. TRAVAUX__ DES FEMMES BELGES)__

ON PEUT SE PROCURER DES BILLETS AU SIÈGE DE L'ALLIANCE FRANCO-BELGE 58, Rue de la Victoire, __ à PARIS.__

PRÉSIDENTS D'HONNEUR__ DE L'ALLIANCE FRANCO-BELGE S.E. le Baron GUILLAUME, Ministre Plénipotentiaire de S.M. le Roi des Belges à Paris__ M. Louis BARTHOU, Député, ancien Président du Conseil des Ministres M. Emile VANDERVELDE, Ministre d'Etat de Belgique__ VICE PRÉSIDENT D'HONNEUR : M. DALIMIER, Sous-Secrétaire d'Etat au Ministère des Beaux-Arts.__ PRÉSIDENT :__ M. STEEG, Sénateur, ancien Ministre.

I. LAPINA, Imp. PARIS.

12 SEPTEMBRE 1915

JOURNÉE DE L'ŒUVRE NIVERNAISE DES MUTILÉS DE LA GUERRE

DEVAMBEZ Imp⁺ PARIS

Neumont, Maurice
1868–1930

12 SEPTEMBRE 1915.
JOURNÉE DE L'ŒUVRE
NIVERNAISE DES
MUTILÉS DE LA GUERRE.

(12 September 1915.
Nivernaise Work Day
for the War Disabled.)

France 1915.
120 × 80 cm.

Chavannaz, B.

UNION DES COLONIES
ÉTRANGÈRES EN
FRANCE EN FAVEUR DES
VICTIMES DE LA
GUERRE....

(Union of the Foreign
Colonies in France for
the Benefit of the
Victims of the War.)

France 1914–1918.

122 × 81 cm.

Picard, G.

JOURNÉE DE PARIS. 14 JUILLET 1915. AU PROFIT DES ŒUVRES DE GUERRE DE L'HOTEL-DE-VILLE POUR LES COMBATTANTS … LES BLESSÉS … LES CONVALESCENTS … LES MUTILÉS … LES REFUGIÉS … LES PRISONNIERS.

(Paris Day. 14 July 1915. For the Benefit of the Town Hall War Work for the Fighters … the Wounded … the Convalescent … the Disabled … the Refugees … the Prisoners.)
France 1915.
120 × 80 cm.

Steinlen, Théophile
Alexandre

1859–1923

OFFICE DE
RENSEIGNEMENTS POUR
LES FAMILLES
DISPERSÉES. . . .

(Office of Information
for Displaced
Families. . . .)

France 1915.

90 × 62 cm mounted
on cloth 110 × 82
cm.

Battermann, W.

ALTONAER
KRIEGSHILFETAG, 29.
SEPT. 1917....
(Altonaer War Relief
Day, 29 Sept.
1917....)
Germany 1917.
68 × 48 cm.

H. R. E.
[Erdt, Hans Rudi]
1883–1918

SOLL UND HABEN DES
KRIEGS-JAHRES 1917 IN
DEN UNION-THEATERN.

(Debit and Credit of
the War Year 1917 in
the Union-Theater.)

Germany [1917].
73 X 95 cm.

GUTE BÜCHER—GUTE
KAMERADEN. GIBST
DU AUCH OFT UND
VIELERLEI: EIN GUTES
BUCH SEI STETS DABEI!

(Good Books—Good
Companions. Give
both Frequently and in
Great Variety: A Good
Book Is Forever.)
Germany [1916].
90 × 60 cm.

Kirchbach, Georg

PALAST-THEATER AM
ZOO ... ZWEI BLAUE
JUNGEN. . . .

(Palast-Theater at the
Zoo ... Two Boys in
Blue. . . .)

Germany [1917].
71 × 96 cm.

Rother, A.

KRIEGSGEFANGEN IN
RUSSLAND. DREI
ABENTEUER-BÜCHER. . . .

(Prisoners of War in
Russia. Three
Adventure Books. . . .)
Germany 1914–1918.
110 × 49 cm.

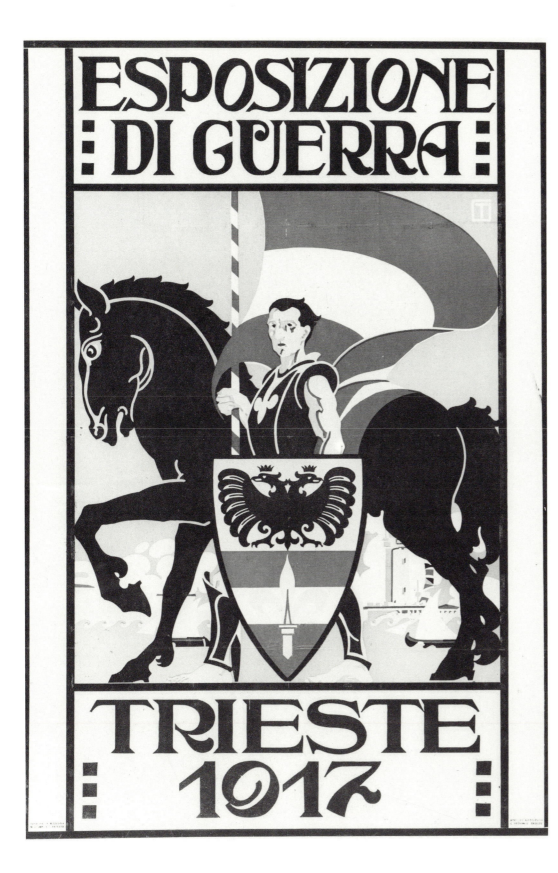

Petronio, G.

ESPOSIZIONE DI
GUERRA. TRIESTE 1917.

(War Exhibition.
Trieste 1917.)
Italy [1917].
100 × 64 cm.

Ost, A.

CONCERT DE CHARITÉ ORGANISÉ LE 17 MARS 1916 AU THÉÂTRE DU SEINPOST À SCHEVENINGUE AU PROFIT DE PHALANSTÈRE BELGE DE KATWYK ET AIDE AUX SOLDATS....

(Charity Concert Organized 17 March 1916 at the Seinpost Theater at Scheveningen for the Benefit of the Belgian Phalanstère of Katwyk and Aid for Soldiers. ...)

Netherlands [1916]. 76 × 104 cm.

Ost, A.

SMOCKING CLUB
AMERSFOORT. . . .

(Amersfoort Smoking
Club. . . .)

Netherlands [1917].

110 × 80 cm.

M. H.

HELPT DEZE VLEK
VERWIJDEREN: STEUNT
HET PRINS BERNHARD
COMITE.

(Help This Spot
Disappear: Support
the Prince Bernhard
Committee.)

Netherlands Antilles
1914–1918?
91 × 60 cm.

SIDE BY SIDE~
BRITANNIA!

Britain's Day Dec. 7th 1918

**Flagg, James
Montgomery**
1877–1960

SIDE BY SIDE—
BRITANNIA! BRITAIN'S
DAY DEC. 7TH 1918.

United States 1918.
68 × 51 cm.

Spear, Gil

WORKERS. Y.M.C.A. LEND YOUR STRENGTH TO THE RED TRIANGLE. HELP THE "Y" HELP THE FIGHTERS FIGHT. UNITED WAR WORK CAMPAIGN —NOVEMBER 11 TO 18.

United States
1915–1918.
70 × 51 cm.

KNOWLEDGE WINS

PUBLIC LIBRARY BOOKS ARE FREE

AMERICAN LIBRARY ASSOCIATION

Smith, Dan
1865–1934

KNOWLEDGE WINS.
PUBLIC LIBRARY BOOKS
ARE FREE.

United States
1915–1918.
72 × 49 cm.

Matania, Fortunino
1881–1963

"HELP THE HORSE TO
SAVE THE SOLDIER."
PLEASE JOIN THE
AMERICAN RED STAR
ANIMAL RELIEF. . . .

United States
1915–1918.
77 × 53 cm.

Ding, J. N.

TIRED OF GIVING? *YOU DON'T KNOW WHAT IT IS TO BE TIRED!...*

United States
1914–1918.
70 × 55 cm.

49

Bettsbain, E. F.

LEST WE PERISH.
CAMPAIGN FOR
$30,000,000. AMERICAN
COMMITTEE FOR RELIEF
IN THE NEAR EAST.
ARMENIA—GREECE—
SYRIA—PERSIA. . . .

United States
1914–1918.
72 × 52 cm.

Falls, C. B.
[Charles Buckles]
1874–1960

NOW FOR SOME MUSIC.
DRAFT YOUR SLACKER
RECORDS. THEY WILL
GO TO CAMP OR
OVERSEAS THROUGH
THE NATIONAL
PHONOGRAPH-
RECORDS RECRUITING
CORPS.

United States
1915–1918.
73 × 49 cm.

Ashe, E. M.

AFTER THE WELCOME
HOME—A JOB!

United States [1919?].
105 × 73 cm.

Falls, C. B.
[Charles Buckles]
1874–1960

BOOKS WANTED FOR
OUR MEN "IN CAMP
AND OVER THERE." TAKE
YOUR GIFTS TO THE
PUBLIC LIBRARY.

United States
1915–1918.
108 × 73 cm.

Foringer, Alonzo Earl

1878–1948

THE GREATEST MOTHER IN THE WORLD. RED CROSS CHRISTMAS ROLL CALL DEC. 16–23RD.

United States 1918. 109 × 72 cm.

54

"I Summon you to Comradeship in the Red Cross"
Woodrow Wilson

Fisher, Harrison
1875–1934

"I SUMMON YOU TO COMRADESHIP IN THE RED CROSS"
—WOODROW WILSON.

United States 1918.
102 × 77 cm.

"THEY SHALL NOT PERISH
CAMPAIGN *for* $30.000.000
AMERICAN COMMITTEE
FOR RELIEF IN THE NEAR EAST
ARMENIA~GREECE~SYRIA~PERSIA

Volk, Douglas
1856–1935

"THEY SHALL NOT
PERISH." CAMPAIGN FOR
$30,000,000. AMERICAN
COMMITTEE FOR RELIEF
IN THE NEAR EAST.
ARMENIA—GREECE—
SYRIA—PERSIA.

United States [1918].
104 × 77 cm.

FORWARD AMERICA !

Kelly, Carroll

FORWARD AMERICA!

United States 1917.

57 × 40 cm.

Bonnerot, Jean

1882– [A. Rapeno]

HERO LAND, OR OVER
THE TOP WITH UNCLE
SAM AND HIS ALLIES.
FOR BENEFIT OF
DEPENDENTS OF
SOLDIERS FROM
AMERICA AND FOR
ALLIED WAR RELIEF. . . .

United States
1917–1918.

57 × 36 cm.

KNITTING FOR
THE NAVY. . . .

United States
1915–1918.
61 × 45 cm.

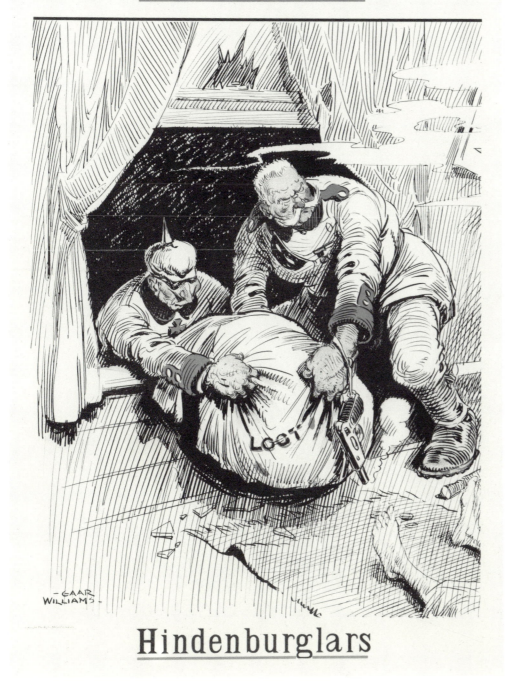

Williams, Gaar
1881–1935
KEEPING UP WITH
WILLIAM . . .
HINDENBURGLARS.
United States
1915–1918.
62 × 37 cm.

Grant, Gordon

1875–1962

LOYALTY TO ONE
MEANS LOYALTY
TO BOTH.

United States
1915–1918.

61 × 46 cm.

Loyalty To One Means
Loyalty To Both

Conservation

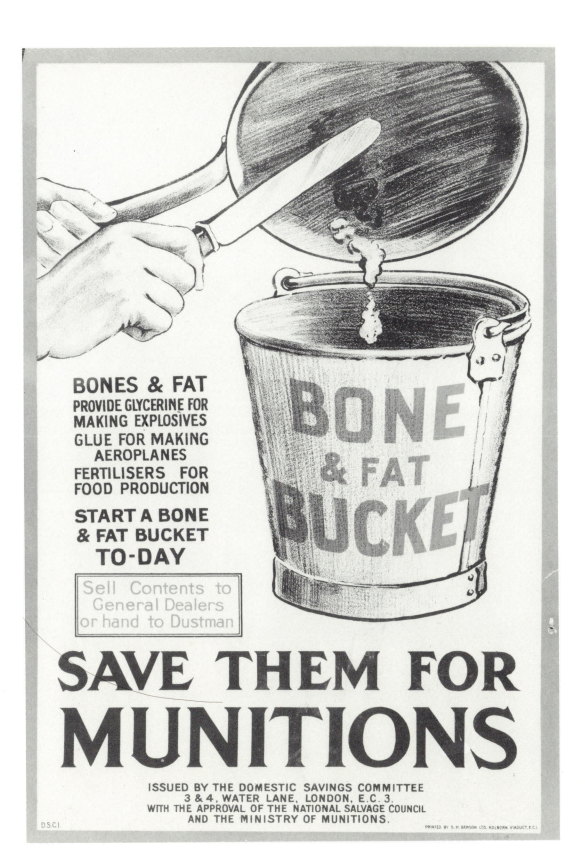

BONE & FAT BUCKET . . .
SAVE THEM FOR
MUNITIONS. . . .

England 1914–1918.
42 × 28 cm.

THE KITCHEN IS THE
[KEY] TO VICTORY.
EAT LESS BREAD.

England 1914–1918.
77 × 51 cm.

Beadle, J. P.

WE RISK OUR LIVES TO
BRING YOU FOOD. IT'S
UP TO YOU NOT TO
WASTE IT. "A MESSAGE
FROM OUR SEAMEN."

England 1917.
77 × 51 cm.

We risk our lives to bring you food.
It's up to you not to
waste it.

"A Message from our Seamen"

DO *YOUR* BIT

SAVE·FOOD

Randall, Maurice

DO *YOUR* BIT.
SAVE FOOD.

England 1914–1918.
77 × 51 cm.

Haulor

SEMEZ DES POMMES DE
TERRE. POUR LES
SOLDATS. POUR LA
FRANCE. . . .

(Plant Potatoes. For
the Soldiers. For
France. . . .)
France 1914–1918.
106 × 76 cm.

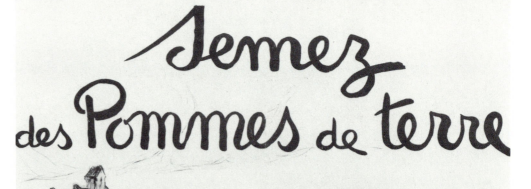

Haulor

FRANÇAIS! LAISSEZ LE CHARBON POUR LES USINES DE GUERRE. BRÛLEZ DE LA TOURBE....

(Frenchmen! Leave the Charcoal for the War Plants. Burn Coke....)
France 1914–1918.
120 × 81 cm.

Verrees, J. Paul

1889–

CAN VEGETABLES,
FRUIT—AND THE
KAISER TOO. . . .

United States 1918.
53 × 36 cm.

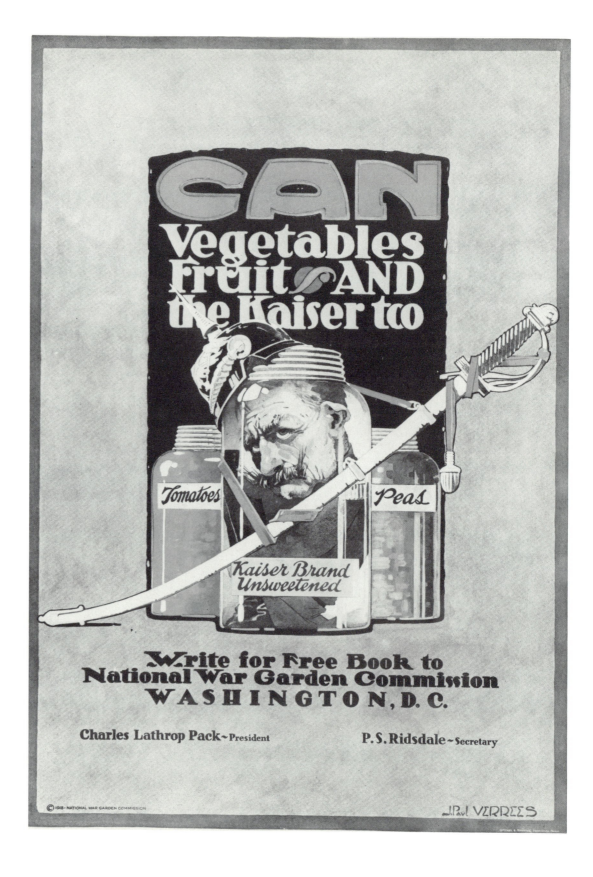

BLOOD or BREAD

Others are giving their blood
You will shorten the war—
save life if you eat only what
you need, and waste nothing.

No.16 UNITED STATES FOOD ADMINISTRATION

Raleigh, Henry
1880–

BLOOD OR BREAD.
OTHERS ARE GIVING
THEIR BLOOD. YOU
WILL SHORTEN THE
WAR—SAVE LIFE IF YOU
EAT ONLY WHAT YOU
NEED, AND WASTE
NOTHING. UNITED
STATES FOOD
ADMINISTRATION.

United States
1917–1918.
74 × 54 cm.

FIGHT WORLD FAMINE.
ENROLL IN THE BOYS'
WORKING RESERVE....

United States
1915–1918.
71 × 49 cm.

UNCLE SAM NEEDS THAT

NEEDS

THAT

EXTRA
SHOVELFUL

Help Uncle Sam to Win the War
by following these Directions:

1. Fire small amounts of coal often.
2. Keep fuel bed even by putting coal on thin spots. Avoid raking and slicing.
3. Keep fuel bed about six inches thick.
4. Look out for air leaks in brickwork.
5. Increase or decrease steam pressure by opening or closing draft damper in uptake.
6. Clean fires when the demand for steam is small, and while cleaning have the draft damper partly closed.

UNITED STATES FUEL ADMINISTRATION

Sindelar, F.

UNCLE SAM NEEDS THAT EXTRA SHOVELFUL. HELP UNCLE SAM TO WIN THE WAR BY FOLLOWING THESE DIRECTIONS . . . UNITED STATES FUEL ADMINISTRATION.

United States
1917–1918.
72 × 52 cm.

80

Mora, F. Luis

1874–1940

DON'T LET UP.
KEEP ON SAVING FOOD.
UNITED STATES FOOD
ADMINISTRATION.

United States
1917–1918.
54 × 36 cm.

FATS ARE FUEL
FOR FIGHTERS. BAKE—
BOIL—AND BROIL
MORE—FRY LESS.
UNITED STATES FOOD
ADMINISTRATION.

United States
1917–1918.
28 × 54 cm.

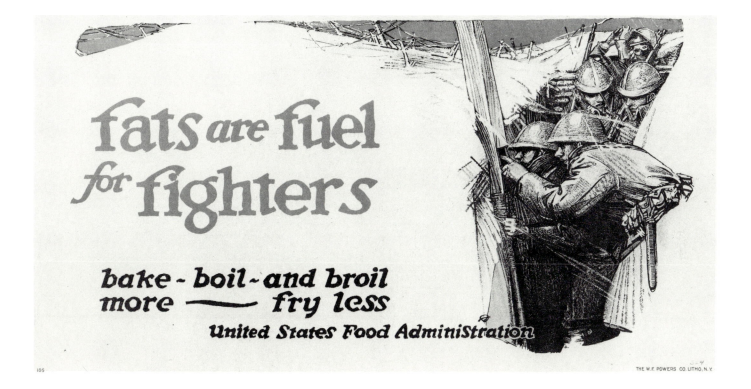

Little AMERICANS
Do your bit

Eat Corn meal mush-
Oatmeal-Corn flakes
Hominy and rice with
milk. *Eat no wheat
cereals.*

Leave nothing on your plate

UNITED STATES FOOD ADMINISTRATION

No. OA

THE WAR AT HOME....
United States
1917–1918.
54 × 31 cm.

Steele

DEFEAT THE KAISER AND HIS U-BOATS. VICTORY DEPENDS ON WHICH FAILS FIRST, FOOD OR FRIGHTFULNESS. EAT LESS WHEAT. . . .

United States
1917–1918.
55 × 36 cm.

Propaganda

Raul

ALERTA! PALAVRAS DO CHEFE DA NAÇÃO. ESTEJAM TODAS AS ATTENÇÕES ALERTA AOS MANEJOS DA ESPIONAGEM, QUE É MULTIFORME. EMMUDEÇAM TODAS AS BOCCAS QUANDO SE TRATAR DE INTERESSE NACIONAL.

(Attention! This is the Head of the Nation. Watch out for the many forms of espionage. All mouths should be shut regarding issues of national interest.)

Brazil 1915–1918.
57 × 77 cm.

Raven-Hill, Leonard
1867–1942
THE GREATER GAME....
England 1914.
77 × 51 cm.

"PUNCH," OCTOBER 21, 1914.

THE GREATER GAME.

MR. PUNCH (*to Professional Association Player*). "NO DOUBT YOU CAN MAKE MONEY IN THIS FIELD, MY FRIEND, BUT THERE'S ONLY ONE FIELD TO-DAY WHERE YOU CAN GET HONOUR."

**Brangwyn, Frank,
Sir**

1867–1956

THE ZEPPELIN RAIDS:
THE VOW OF
VENGEANCE. DRAWN
FOR "THE DAILY
CHRONICLE" BY FRANK
BRANGWYN A.R.A.
"DAILY CHRONICLE"
READERS ARE COVERED
AGAINST THE RISKS OF
BOMBARDMENT BY
ZEPPELIN OR
AEROPLANE.

England 1914–1918.
77 × 51 cm.

RUMANIA'S DAY....
England 1914–1918.
77 × 51 cm.

Wilson, David

1873–1935

W. F. B.

WHAT A RED RAG IS TO
A BULL—THE RED CROSS
IS TO THE HUN. . . .

England 1914–1918.

77 × 51 cm.

WHAT A RED RAG IS TO A BULL-

THE RED CROSS IS TO THE HUN.

To the already Long List of Outrages by the HUNS on The RED CROSS both on Land and Sea, there was added on January the 4th This Year, the Sinking without warning in the Bristol Channel of the Hospital Ship "REWA."—Fortunately owing to the Splendid Discipline and the Unselfish and Heroic Conduct of the Officers, Crew, and The Medical Staff, All the wounded, of whom there were over 700 on board were saved,—But three poor Lascar Firemen went down with the ship.

THE DANGERFIELD PRINTING CO. LTD. LONDON

RED CROSS OR IRON CROSS?

WOUNDED AND A PRISONER
OUR SOLDIER CRIES FOR WATER.

THE GERMAN "SISTER"
POURS IT ON THE GROUND BEFORE HIS EYES.

THERE IS NO WOMAN IN BRITAIN
WHO WOULD DO IT.

THERE IS NO WOMAN IN BRITAIN
WHO WILL FORGET IT.

THE DANGERFIELD PRINTING CO. LTD. LONDON

Wilson, David
1873–1935
W. F. B.

RED CROSS OR IRON CROSS? WOUNDED AND A PRISONER, OUR SOLDIER CRIES FOR WATER. THE GERMAN "SISTER" POURS IT ON THE GROUND BEFORE HIS EYES. THERE IS NO WOMAN IN BRITAIN WHO WOULD DO IT. THERE IS NO WOMAN IN BRITAIN WHO WILL FORGET IT.

England 1914–1918.
77 × 51 cm.

"KNIGHTS OF THE AIR"

LOOK HINDENBURG! MY GERMAN HEROES!

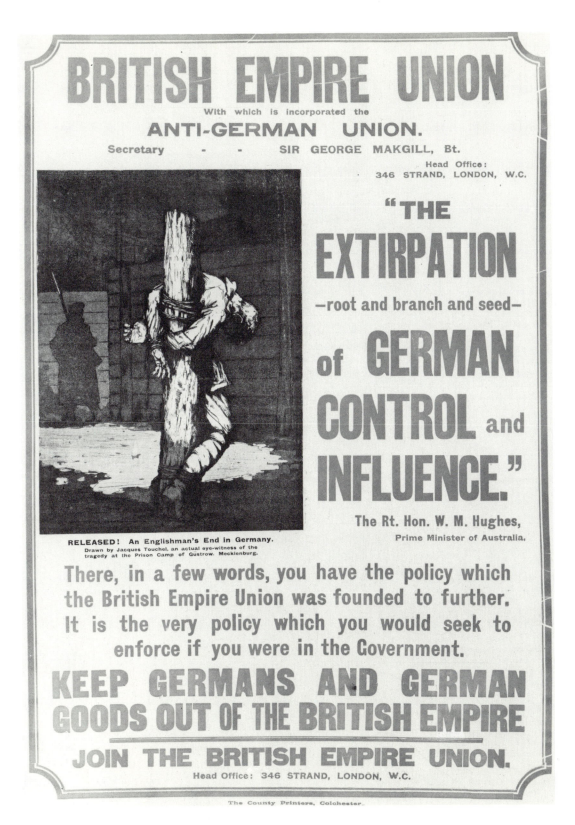

BRITISH EMPIRE UNION, WITH WHICH IS INCORPORATED THE ANTI-GERMAN UNION. . . . "THE EXTIRPATION—ROOT AND BRANCH AND SEED—OF GERMAN CONTROL AND INFLUENCE." . . . KEEP GERMANS AND GERMAN GOODS OUT OF THE BRITISH EMPIRE. JOIN THE BRITISH EMPIRE UNION. . . .

England 1914–1918. 77 × 51 cm.

SOUVENEZ-VOUS DE LA
BELGIQUE ET DU NORD
DE LA FRANCE.
N'ACHETEZ RIEN AUX
BOCHES.

(Remember Belgium
and the North of
France. Buy Nothing
German.)

England 1914–1918.

77 × 51 cm.

Wilson, David
1873–1935
W. F. B.

BRITISH EMPIRE UNION.
"ONCE A GERMAN—
ALWAYS A GERMAN!" …
England 1914–1918.
77 × 51 cm.

Muller, E.

N'OUBLIONS JAMAIS.
LEST WE FORGET. PATHÉ.

France 1918.
120 × 81 cm.

DER ALTE KAMPF
BEGINNT AUFS NEU',
NUN, DEUTSCHER,
SEIDEM DEUTSCHEN
TREU! BILDET DEUTSCHE
VOLKSRÄTE!

(The Old Fight Begins
Anew, Now, Germans,
Be True to Germany!
Build the German
Popular Government!)
Germany 1914–1918.
59 × 44 cm.

BONDS—WHICH?

Cesare, O. E.
BONDS—WHICH?
United States
1915–1918.
56 × 36 cm.

Recruiting

AUSTRALIA HAS
PROMISED BRITAIN
50,000 MORE MEN.
WILL YOU HELP US
KEEP THAT PROMISE?

Australia 1914–1918.
64 × 103 cm.

LES HEROS DE ST.-JULIEN
ET DE FESTUBERT...
SUIVRONS-NOUS LEUR
EXEMPLE? S'ADRESSER
AU BUREAU DE
RECRUTEMENT.

(The Heros of St.-
Julien and Festubert...
Shall We Follow Their
Example? Report to
the Recruitment
Bureau.)
Canada 1914–1918.
94 × 63 cm.

110

BRITONS

"WANTS YOU"

JOIN YOUR COUNTRY'S ARMY!

GOD SAVE THE KING

Reproduced by permission of LONDON OPINION

Printed by the Victoria House Printing Co., Ltd., Tudor Street, London, E.C.

Leete, Alfred
1882–1933

BRITONS, [LORD KITCHENER] "WANTS YOU." JOIN YOUR COUNTRY'S ARMY! GOD SAVE THE KING.

England [1914].
77 × 51 cm.

AT NEUVE CHAPELLE

YOUR FRIENDS NEED YOU. BE A MAN

DESIGNED AND LITHOGRAPHED BY FRANK BRANGWYN. ARA.   PRINTED BY THE AVENUE PRESS L.^{TD} BOUVERIE S.^T LONDON. ENG.

**Brangwyn, Frank,
Sir**
1867–1956
AT NEUVE CHAPELLE
YOUR FRIENDS NEED
YOU. BE A MAN.
England 1914–1918.
77 × 51 cm.

**Baden-Powell of
Gilwell, Baron
(Robert Stephenson
Smyth Baden-
Powell)**

1857–1941

ARE YOU IN THIS?

England 1914–1918.
77 × 50 cm.

Low, Baron (David Low)
1891–196–?

EVERYONE SHOULD DO HIS BIT. ENLIST NOW.

England 1915.
77 × 51 cm.

115

BRITAIN NEEDS YOU
AT ONCE.

England 1914–1918.
77 × 51 cm.

116

Daddy, what did <u>YOU</u> do in the Great War?

Lumley, Savile
DADDY, WHAT DID *YOU*
DO IN THE GREAT WAR?
England 1914–1918.
77 × 51 cm.

THE VETERAN'S FAREWELL.

"Good Bye, my lad,
I only wish I were young enough
to go with you!"

ENLIST NOW!

TAKE UP THE SWORD OF JUSTICE

Partridge, J.
Bernard, Sir
1861–1945

TAKE UP THE SWORD
OF JUSTICE.
England [1915].
77 × 51 cm.

Kemp-Welch, Lucy Elizabeth
1869–1958

FORWARD! FORWARD TO VICTORY. ENLIST NOW.

England 1915.
77 × 51 cm.

Kealey, E. V.

WOMEN OF BRITAIN
SAY—"GO!"

England 1915.
77 × 51 cm.

"BE HONEST WITH YOURSELF. BE CERTAIN THAT YOUR SO-CALLED REASON IS NOT A SELFISH EXCUSE"
LORD KITCHENER

ENLIST TO-DAY

"BE HONEST WITH YOURSELF. BE CERTAIN THAT YOUR SO-CALLED REASON IS NOT A SELFISH EXCUSE." LORD KITCHENER. ENLIST TO-DAY.
England 1914–1918.
77 × 51 cm.

Carlu, Jacques

PASSANT! FAIS TOUT
TON DEVOIR . . . ,—SI JE
ME DÉROBAIS AU
MIEN, COMMENT
M'APPELLERAIS-TU?

(Who Goes There?
Do Your Duty . . . ,—If
I Shirked Mine, What
Would You Call Me?)

France 1917.
66 × 93 cm.

Delaspre, H.

L'INFANTERIE FRANÇAISE
DANS LA BATAILLE.

(The French Infantry
in Battle.)

France 1914–1918.

120 × 80 cm.

WILL YOU MAKE
A FOURTH ?

WILL YOU MAKE
A FOURTH?
Ireland 1914–1918.
77 × 51 cm.

AN IRISH HERO! *ONE IRISHMAN DEFEATS 10 GERMANS. SERGEANT MICHAEL O'LEARY, V.C. IRISH GUARDS. HAVE YOU NO WISH TO EMULATE THE SPLENDID BRAVERY OF YOUR FELLOW COUNTRYMAN? JOIN AN IRISH REGIMENT TO-DAY.*

Ireland 1915.
77 × 51 cm.

Can You any longer resist the Call?

CAN YOU ANY LONGER
RESIST THE CALL?

Ireland 1914–1918.
77 × 51 cm.

130

CABLED APPEAL FOR DRAFTS

"The success of the South African Brigade at Messines Ridge is one of the glories of the War."

"As a unit their reputation is almost unrivalled. I trust sufficient Drafts will be sent forward."

SMUTS.

Wants You.

Holland, A.

CABLED APPEAL FOR DRAFTS.... J. C. SMUTS WANTS *YOU*.

South Africa
1914–1918.
103 × 64 cm.

Coughlin, John A.
FIRST IN FRANCE.
U.S. MARINES. . . .
United States
1917–1918.
72 × 54 cm.

132

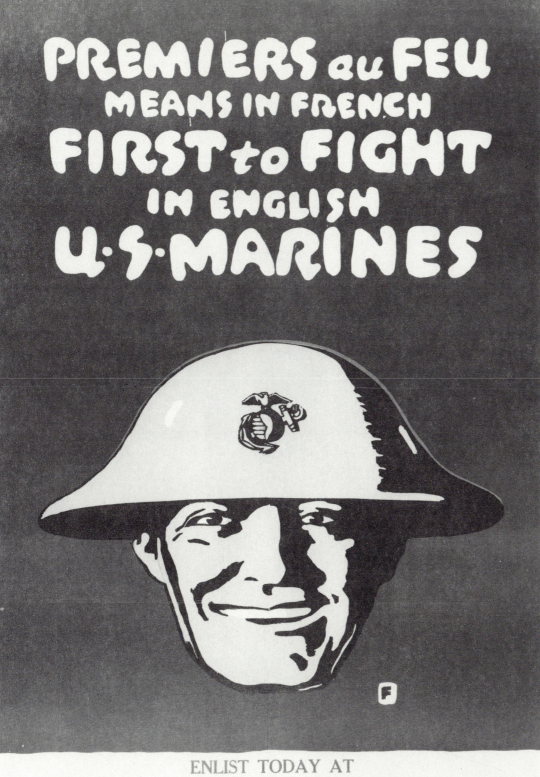

Falls, C. B.
[Charles Buckles]
1874–1960
PREMIERS AU FEU MEANS
IN FRENCH, FIRST TO
FIGHT; IN ENGLISH, U.S.
MARINES. . . .
United States
1917–1918.
107 × 72 cm.

Christy, Howard Chandler

1873–1952

GEE!! I WISH I WERE A MAN. I'D JOIN THE NAVY. BE A MAN AND DO IT. UNITED STATES NAVY RECRUITING STATION.

United States 1917.

104 × 69 cm.

DON'T WAIT for the Draft VOLUNTEER

ASSOCIATED MOTION PICTURE ADVERTISERS, INC. Poster No. 3

GUENTHER

Guenther

DON'T WAIT FOR THE
DRAFT. VOLUNTEER.

United States
1917–1918.
108 × 77 cm.

135

Reuterdahl, Henry
1871–1925

ALL TOGETHER!   United States [1917].
ENLIST IN THE NAVY.   82 × 101 cm.

ENLIST *IN THE* NAVY

Raemaeker, Louis
1869–1956
ENLIST IN THE NAVY.
United States
1917–1918.
72 × 88 cm.

137

WAKE UP, AMERICA!
CIVILIZATION CALLS
EVERY MAN WOMAN
AND CHILD!...

United States 1917.
108 × 72 cm.

138

Moody

EVEN A DOG ENLISTS.
WHY NOT YOU?…

United States
1917–1918.
108 × 73 cm.

Lie, Jonas
1880–

ON THE JOB FOR
VICTORY. UNITED STATES
SHIPPING BOARD
EMERGENCY FLEET
CORPORATION.

United States
1917–1918.
76 × 98 cm.

ON THE JOB FOR VICTORY

UNITED STATES SHIPPING BOARD EMERGENCY FLEET CORPORATION

Welsh

IF YOU ARE AN ELECTRICIAN, MECHANIC OR A TELEGRAPH OPERATOR YOU BELONG IN THE U.S. ARMY SIGNAL CORPS. IF YOU ARE NOT, WE WILL TRAIN YOU. GET IN NOW.

United States
1917–1918.
105 × 72 cm.

[Preissig, Vojtech]

[1873–1944]

CZECHOSLOVAKS! JOIN
OUR FREE COLORS!

United States
1917–1918.
91 × 65 cm.

[Preissig, Vojtech]

[1873–1944]

ZA NAŠISAMOSTATNOST! HRR NA VRAHA! ZA DEMOKRACII! ČESKOSLOVENSKÁ ARMÁDA.

(For Our Independence! Hurry against the Killer! For Democracy! Czechoslovak Army.)

United States 1917–1918.

91 × 65 cm.

Flagg, James Montgomery
1877–1960

I WANT YOU FOR U.S. ARMY. NEAREST RECRUITING STATION.

United States 1917.
104 × 77 cm.

Hutaf, August
William
1879–
TREAT 'EM ROUGH! JOIN
THE TANKS. UNITED
STATES TANK CORPS.
OPEN TO FIGHTING
MEN. ALL CLASSES 18 TO
45. SEE RECRUITING
OFFICER AT ADOLPHUS
HOTEL.
United States
1917–1918.
57 × 35 cm.

**Flagg, James
Montgomery**
1877–1960

SOME BACKING! THE
EMPIRE STATE NEEDS
SOLDIERS. JOIN THE
NEW YORK STATE
GUARD!

United States
1917–1918.
56 × 28 cm.

War Loan

She gave all — *You buy*

LATE
NURSE CAVELL

PEACE
BONDS

LATE NURSE CAVELL.
SHE GAVE ALL—*YOU* BUY
PEACE BONDS.

Australia 1914–1918.
77 × 51 cm.

Karpellus, Adolph

1869–1919

ZEICHNET VIERTE ÖSTERREICHISCHE KRIEGSANLEIHE. KAIS. KÖN. PRIVILEGIRTE ÖSTERREICHISCHE LÄNDERBANK.

(Subscribe to the Fourth Austrian War Loan. . . .)

Austria 1914–1918.
95 × 64 cm.

ZEICHNET 6ᵗᵉ KRIEGSANLEIHE

WILLY STIEBORSKY

EIN JEDER LEISTE DAS SEINE ZUM GUTEN ENDE!

WIENER KOMMERZIAL-BANK

1. Kohlmarkt 8

Stieborsky, Willy

ZEICHNET 6TE
KRIEGSANLEIHE.
EIN JEDER LEISTE
DAS SEINE ZUM GUTEN
ENDE! WIENER
KOMMERZIAL-BANK.
1 KOHLMARKT 8.

(Subscribe to the
6th War Loan. Each
Produces His Own
Good End! . . .)
Austria [1917?].
96 × 63 cm.

Libesny, Kurt

ZEICHNET OESTERR.
8 KRIEGSANLEIHE!
ANMELDUNGEN NIMMT
DIE ANGLO OESTERR.
BANK ENTGEGEN.

(Subscribe to the
8th Austrian War
Loan. Registration
Accepted at the
Anglo-Austrian Bank.)
Austria [1918].
96 × 63 cm.

154

ELLES SERVENT LA
FRANCE. TOUT LE
MONDE PEUT SERVIR.
SOUSCRIVONS À
L'EMPRUNT DE LA
VICTOIRE.

(They Serve France.
Everyone Can Serve.
Let's Subscribe to the
Victory Loan.)

Canada 1914–1918.
90 × 62 cm.

LEND YOUR FIVE
SHILLINGS TO YOUR
COUNTRY AND CRUSH
THE GERMANS.

England [1915].

77 × 51 cm.

Poulbot, Francisque
1879–1946

EMPRUNT DE LA
DÉFENSE NATIONALE.
—N'OUBLIE PAS DE
SOUSCRIRE . . . POUR LA
VICTOIRE! . . . ET LE
RETOUR! . . .

(National Defense
Loan.—Don't Forget
to Subscribe . . . For
Victory! . . . And Their
Return! . . .)

France 1915.
114 × 80 cm.

158

L'EMPRUNT
DES
"DERNIÈRES
CARTOUCHES"

FRANÇAIS,
ENCORE UN EFFORT..!

TEL

publié par "l'Agenda Financier" – 50, rue Notre-Dame des Victoires Paris

LES ÉDITIONS D'ART 186 Rue de Rivoli PARIS, visa 944

Tel

L'EMPRUNT DES "DERNIÈRES CARTOUCHES." FRANÇAIS, ENCORE UN EFFORT..!
(Loan of the "Last Trenches." Frenchmen, Yet Another Try..!)
France 1914–1918.
119 × 81 cm.

POUR LA FRANCE VERSEZ VOTRE OR

L'Or Combat Pour La Victoire

Faivre, Abel
1867–1945

POUR LA FRANCE,
VERSEZ VOTRE OR.
L'OR COMBAT POUR
LA VICTOIRE.

(For France, Turn over
Your Gold. Gold Fights
for Victory.)

France 1915.
121 × 81 cm.

Jonas, Lucien

1880–1947

EMPRUNT DE LA
LIBÉRATION.
SOUSCRIVEZ. STÉ. GLE.
DE CRÉDIT INDUSTRIEL
& COMMERCIAL. 66, RUE
DE LA VICTOIRE—PARIS.

(Liberation Loan.
Subscribe. . . .)

France [1918].

120 × 80 cm.

Barbier, Antoine
1859–

COMITÉ DE L'OR DU
DÉPARTEMENT DU
RHÔNE. POUR LA PATRIE
VERSEZ VOTRE OR.

(Gold Committee of
the Département du
Rhône. Turn over
Your Gold for the
Country.)
France 1914–1918.
120 × 85 cm.

163

Faivre, Abel

1867–1945

CRÉDIT LYONNAIS. SOUSCRIVEZ AU 4E EMPRUNT NATIONAL.

(Crédit Lyonnais. Subscribe to the 4th National Loan.)

France [1918]. 79 × 120 cm.

Chavannaz, B.

EMPRUNT DE LA
LIBÉRATION 1918.
SOUSCRIVEZ!
BONBRIGHT & CO. 9,
RUE ST. FLORENTIN,
PARIS.

(1918 Liberation Loan.
Subscribe!...)

France 1918.

112 × 81 cm.

Faivre, Abel

1867–1945

3E EMPRUNT DE LA DÉFENSE NATIONALE. CRÉDIT LYONNAIS. SOUSCRIVEZ.

(3rd National Defense Loan. Crédit Lyonnais. Subscribe.)

France [1917?].
120 × 81 cm.

Falter, M.

POUR LE SUPRÊME
EFFORT. EMPRUNT
NATIONAL. SOCIÉTÉ
GÉNÉRALE.

(For the Last Try.
National Loan. Société
Générale.)
France 1918.
121 × 81 cm.

Chavannaz, B.

EMPRUNT NATIONAL 1918. SOCIÉTÉ GÉNÉRALE. POUR NOUS RENDRE ENTIÈRE LA DOUCE TERRE DE FRANCE.

(1918 National Loan. Société Générale. To Return Whole to Us the Sweet Land of France.)

France [1918]. 80 × 120 cm.

Baste

BANQUE INDUSTRIELLE
DE CHINE. 74, RUE ST.-
LAZARE, PARIS. 4E
EMPRUNT NATIONAL.

(Industrial Bank of
China. 74, Rue St.-
Lazare, Paris. 4th
National Loan.)

France 1918.
119 × 81 cm.

Erler, Fritz

1868–1940

UND IHR? ZEICHNET
KRIEGSANLEIHE.

(And You? Subscribe
to the War Loan.)

Germany 1914–1918.

58 × 43 cm.

Erler, Fritz

1868–1940

DER 9TE PFEIL. ZEICHNET
KRIEGSANLEIHE.

(The 9th Arrow.
Subscribe to the
War Loan.)
Germany [1917?].
58 × 44 cm.

171

Bernhard, Lucien
1883–1972

DAS IST DER WEG
ZUM FRIEDEN—DIE
FEINDE WOLLEN ES
SO! DARUM ZEICHNE
KRIEGSANLEIHE!

(This Is the Path
toward Peace—The
Enemy Wishes It So!
Therefore Subscribe
to the War Loan!)
Germany 1914–1918.
65 × 47 cm.

Er schützt uns Haus und Hof darum zeichnet Kriegsanleihe!

ER SCHÜTZT UNS
HAUS UND HOF.
DARUM ZEICHNET
KRIEGSANLEIHE!
(He [Hindenburg]
Protects House and
Home. Therefore
Subscribe to the War
Loan!)
Germany 1914–1918.
95 × 60 cm.

Pap, Mich

ENTOKA TAMEIAKA
GRAMMATIA 5%....
(5% War Loan....)
Greece 1914–1918.
84 × 58 cm.

SEGITSETEK A DIADALMAS BÉKÉHEZ

JEGYEZZÜNK HADIKÖLCSÖNT

SEGITSETEK A
DIADALMAS BÉKÉHEZ.
JEGYEZZÜNK
HADIKÖLCSÖNT.

(Help for a Victorious
Peace. Register for the
War Loan.)

Hungary 1917.
96 × 64 cm.

Mauzan, Luciano Achille

1883–

FATE TUTTI IL VOSTRO DOVERE! LE SOTTOSCRIZIONI AL PRESTITO....

(Do Your Whole Duty! The Subscription to the War Loan....)

Italy 1914–1918.

101 × 70 cm.

Borgoni, Mario
1869–

PRESTITO NAZIONALE
RENDITA CONSOLIDATA
5% NETTO....

(National Loan 5%
Consolidated Net
Yield....)
Italy 1914–1918.
100 × 70 cm.

PRESTITO NAZIONALE
RENDITA CONSOLIDATA
5% NETTO EMESSA A
L.90 PER 100
NOMINALI....

(National Loan 5%
Consolidated Net
Yield Issued in 90
to 100 Lira
Denominations....)
Italy 1914–1918.
105 × 72 cm.

WAR WEAPONS WEEK.
APRIL 8TH TO 13TH.
HELP TO PROVIDE THIS
WAR WEAPON. BUY
NATIONAL WAR BONDS
(£5 TO £5000) AND WAR
SAVINGS CERTIFICATES
15/6.

Scotland 1918.
77 × 51 cm.

Leyendecker, J. C. [Joseph Christian]
1874–1951

U.S.A. BONDS. THIRD LIBERTY LOAN CAMPAIGN. BOY SCOUTS OF AMERICA. WEAPONS FOR LIBERTY.

United States [1917?].
77 × 52 cm.

W.S.S. PLEDGE WEEK.
HELP HIM BAG THE HUN.
$100 PER FAMILY—$20
PER INDIVIDUAL AT THE
VERY *LEAST!*

United States
1917–1918.
72 × 54 cm.

Raleigh, Henry
1880–

HALT THE HUN! BUY U.S. GOVERNMENT BONDS. THIRD LIBERTY LOAN.

United States [1918].
76 × 51 cm.

Coffin, Haskell

JOAN OF ARC SAVED
FRANCE. WOMEN OF
AMERICA, SAVE YOUR
COUNTRY. BUY WAR
SAVINGS STAMPS.
UNITED STATES
TREASURY DEPARTMENT.

United States
1917–1918.
77 × 52 cm.

Riesenberg,
Sidney H.

LEND AS THEY FIGHT.
BUY MORE LIBERTY
BONDS.

United States [1917].
77 × 52 cm.

Young, Ellsworth

REMEMBER BELGIUM.
BUY BONDS. FOURTH
LIBERTY LOAN.

United States [1918].
77 × 52 cm.

187

REMEMBER! THE FLAG OF
LIBERTY, SUPPORT IT!
BUY U.S. GOVERNMENT
BONDS. 3RD LIBERTY
LOAN.

United States [1917?].
77 × 52 cm.

REMEMBER !
THE FLAG OF LIBERTY
SUPPORT IT !

BUY
U.S. Government Bonds
3rd. LIBERTY LOAN

EVERY LIBERTY BOND IS
A SHOT AT A U BOAT.
FIRE *YOUR* SHOT TO-DAY.
BUY A LIBERTY BOND.
SECOND LIBERTY LOAN.

United States 1917.
28 × 54 cm.

IF YOU DON'T WANT
THIS OVER HERE—BUY
MORE LIBERTY BONDS.
THIRD LIBERTY LOAN.

United States 1917.
28 × 54 cm.

Pennell, Joseph
1857–1926

PROVIDE THE SINEWS
OF WAR. BUY LIBERTY
BONDS.

United States 1918.
51 × 53 cm.

JOSEPH PENNELL.DEL

HEYWOOD STRASSER & VOIGT LITHO. CO. N.Y. IMP.

PROVIDE THE SINEWS OF WAR
BUY LIBERTY BONDS

SWAT THE BRUTES WITH
LIBERTY BONDS.
United States
1917–1918.
46 × 36 cm.

Women

WOMEN ARE WORKING
DAY & NIGHT TO WIN
THE WAR. £25,000
IMMEDIATELY NEEDED
FOR THE WOMEN'S WAR
TIME FUND TO PROVIDE
REST-ROOMS, CANTEENS
& HOSTELS....

England 1914–1918.
77 × 51 cm.

Gawthorn, H. G.

HELP THEM TO CARRY ON. Y.W.C.A. BLUE TRIANGLE WEEK. NOV. 21 TO 28.

England 1918.

77 × 51 cm.

196

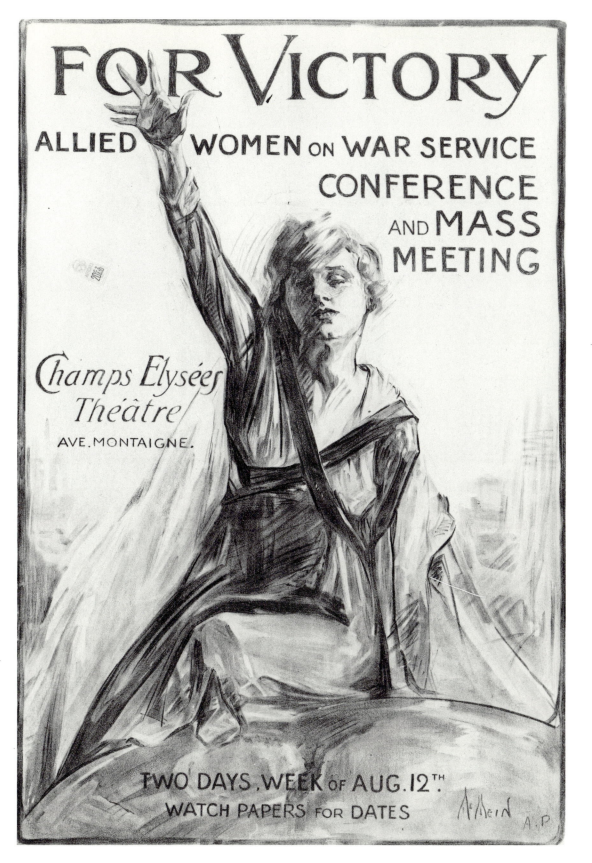

McMein

FOR VICTORY, ALLIED
WOMEN ON WAR
SERVICE CONFERENCE
AND MASS MEETING.
CHAMPS ELYSÉES
THÉÂTRE. AVE.
MONTAIGNE. TWO
DAYS, WEEK OF AUG.
12TH. WATCH PAPERS
FOR DATES.

France [1918?].
120 × 81 cm.

Kirchbach, Georg

DEUTSCHE FRAUEN
ARBEITET IM HEIMAT-
HEER! KRIEGSAMTSTELLE
MAGDEBURG.

(German Women
Work in the Home-
Army! Magdeburg
War Office.)

Germany 1914–1918.
72 × 94 cm.

Paus, Herbert

1880–1946

THE WOMAN'S LAND
ARMY OF AMERICA.
WOMEN ENLIST NOW
AND HELP THE FARMER
FIGHT THE FOOD
FAMINE. . . .

United States 1918.
77 × 52 cm.

Underwood, Clarence F.

1871–1929

BACK OUR Y.W.C.A. GIRLS OVER THERE. UNITED WAR WORK CAMPAIGN.

United States
1917–1918.

77 × 54 cm.

**Flagg, James
Montgomery**
1877–1960
STAGE WOMEN'S
WAR RELIEF.
United States
1914–1918.
78 × 57 cm.

201

Baker, Ernest Hamlin

FOR EVERY FIGHTER, A WOMAN WORKER. Y.W.C.A. BACK OUR SECOND LINE OF DEFENSE. UNITED WAR WORK CAMPAIGN.

United States
1917–1918.
108 × 72 cm.

McMein

ONE OF THE
THOUSAND Y.W.C.A.
GIRLS IN FRANCE.
UNITED WAR WORK
CAMPAIGN NOV. 11TH
TO 18TH.

United States [1918?].
72 × 108 cm.

Jonas, Lucien
1880–1947

FOUR YEARS IN THE
FIGHT. THE WOMEN OF
FRANCE. WE OWE THEM
HOUSES OF CHEER.
UNITED WAR WORK
CAMPAIGN.

United States
1917–1918.
109 × 72 cm.

Patterson, Lucille

SERVICE. FALL IN!
NATIONAL LEAGUE FOR
WOMANS SERVICE.

United States
1917–1918.
64 × 45 cm.

CAN YOU DRIVE A CAR?
WILL YOU DRIVE ONE IN FRANCE?
IMMEDIATE SERVICE AT THE FRONT!

American Field Service

40 State Street   Boston, Mass.

Bibliography

Adams, Herbert. "The War Influence on Art." *Forum* 61 (Jan. 1919): 71–76.

L'Affiche et les Arts de la Publicité (a war posters number, 1928).

Allen, Lafon. "Lafon Allen Collection of Posters of the World War." *Yale University Library Gazette*, July 1937.

American Art Galleries. *Allied War Salon*. Introduction by A. E. Gallatin. New York, 1918. (Catalogue of exhibition, 9–24 Dec. 1918.)

Arden Gallery, New York. *Exhibition of War Posters of the Allied Nations for the Benefit of the American Red Cross, Given under the Auspices of the American Art News and Arden Studios, Inc. December Third to Twenty-second, Inclusive, 1917*. New York: Arden Gallery, 1917.

Art and Industry. 1939–1945. (Serial.)

"Art and the Liberty Loan." *Harper's Bazaar* 53 (Dec. 1918): 30–31.

"The Art Institute's Part in the War." *Chicago Art Bulletin* 11 (May 1917): 314–15.

"Artist Evolves New Poster Letter." *The Poster* 9 (Oct. 1918): 32.

Artists for Victory: An Exhibition Catalog. Prepared by Ellen G. Landau, Case Western Reserve University. Washington, D.C.: U.S. Government Printing Office, 1983.

"The Artist's Share in the Third Liberty Loan Campaign." *Cartoons* 13 (April 1918): 459–62.

Barton, Bruce (Publicity Director). *United War Work Campaign, November 1–18, 1918*. New York, 1918.

Buffalo Fine Arts Academy, Albright Gallery. *Catalogue and Exhibition of War Posters, Drawings and Lithographs, Jan. 12–Feb. 3, 1918*. Buffalo: Albright Gallery, 1918.

Buffalo Fine Arts Academy, Albright Gallery. *Catalogue of an Exhibition of French War Posters Lent by the National City Company, November 12–December 31, 1918*. Buffalo: Albright Gallery, 1918.

"C. D. Gibson's Committee for Patriotic Posters." *New York Times Magazine*, 20 Jan. 1918, sec. 7, p. 11.

Coffey, John Williams. *American Posters of World War One: Catalogue and Exhibition*. Williamstown, Mass.: Williams College Museum of Art, [c. 1978].

Connolly, Louise. *Posters and American War Posters: Historical and Explanatory*. Newark, N.J.: Free Public Library, 1917.

"Contest for Best W.S.S. Posters." *New York Times*, 19 May 1918, sec. 4, p. 2.

Crane, Aimee. *Art in the Armed Forces: Pictured by Men in Action*. New York: Garland Publishing, 1972.

Creel, George. *How We Advertised America*. New York: Harper & Brothers Publishers, 1920.

Darracott, Joseph, ed. *The First World War in Posters*. New York: Dover Publications, 1974.

Darracott, Joseph, and Loftus, Belinda. *First World War Posters*. London, 1972.

Davignon, Henri. *German Posters in Belgium, Their Value as Evidence, New Texts and Documents*. Edinburgh, New York, 1918.

Davignon, Henri. *German Posters in Belgium, Their Value as Evidence, New Texts, and Documents*. London: Thomas Nelson & Sons, 1918.

Downey, Fairfax. *Portrait of an Era as Drawn by C. D. Gibson*. New York: Charles Scribner's Sons, 1936.

Eichenberg, Fritz. *The Art of the Print*. New York: Harry N. Abrams, 1976.

Emerson, Guy. "Harvard Collection of War Posters." *Harvard Alumni Bulletin* 21 (1919): 279–83.

Emerson, R. W. "Posters for Victory Liberty Loan." *The Poster* 10 (May 1919): 18.

An Exhibition of Lithographs of War Work by Joseph Pennell. Exhibited under the Auspices of the American Federation of the Arts, January 5 to 29, 1918, Art Museum, Eden Park. Cincinnati, Ohio: Museum Press, 1918.

Fehl, Philipp. "A Stylistic Analysis of Some Propaganda Posters of World War II." M.A. thesis, Stanford University, 1948.

Fehl, Philipp, and Fenix, Patricia. *World War I Propaganda Posters*. Chapel Hill, 1969.

Fern, Allen. *Word and Image*. New York: Museum of Modern Art, 1969.

Feurlicht, Adoph L. "The Poster's Part in the Great War." *The Poster* 10 (Feb. 1919): 28–31.

Gallatin, Albert Eugene. *Art and the Great War*. New York: E. P. Dutton & Co., 1919.

Gallo, Max. *The Poster in History*. New York: American Heritage Publishing Co., 1972.

Glass, Carter. "Practical Patriotism in American Art." *Art & Life* 10 (June 1919): 295–97.

"Government Asks Artists to Make War Posters."

New York Times Magazine, 20 May 1917, sec. 6, p. 14.

Great Britain Stationery Office. *Catalogue of War Literature Issued by H.M. Government, 1914–1919. Including: Recruiting, War Saving and Other Pictorial Posters, and More Interesting of Numerous Publications Bearing Upon the War, Some of Which Have Not Been Previously Offered for Sale.* London: Great Britain Stationery Office, 1921.

"A Great Esthetic Work . . . Is in the Hands of the Department of Pictorial Publicity." *Chicago Art Institute Bulletin* 12 (May 1918): 76–77.

Hamilton, Clayton. "Posters of the Great War." *Munsey's Magazine* 64 (June 1918): 37–64.

Hardie, Martin, and Sabin, Arthur K. *War Posters, Issued by Belligerent and Neutral Nations 1914–1919.* London: A. & C. Black, 1920.

Harper, Paula. *War Revolution and Peace.* Palo Alto: Stanford University Museum of Art, 1971.

Hillier, Bevis. *Posters.* New York: Stein & Day, 1969.

Honing, William A., Private, U.S.M.C. "War Posters: Are Silent and Powerful Recruiters." *Recruiters Bulletin*, August 1917, pp. 4–5.

Hutchinson, Harold F. *The Poster: An Illustrated History from 1860.* New York: Viking Press, 1968.

Images of the Great War: 1914–1918. Curated by Gordon L. Fuglie. Edited by Lucinda H. Gedeon. 26 April 1983 to 29 May 1983. Los Angeles: Grunwald Center for the Graphic Arts, Dickson Art Center, University of California, [1983].

Joseph Pennell's Pictures of War Work in America: Reproductions of a Series of Lithographs of the United States Government, with Notes and an Introduction by the Artist. Philadelphia, London: J. B. Lippincott Company, 1918.

Joseph Pennell's Pictures of War Work in England: Reproductions of a Series of Drawings and Lithographs of the Munition Works Made by Him with the Permission and Authority of the British Government, with Notes by the Artist and an Introduction by H. G. Wells. London: Heinemann, 1917.

Judd, Denis. *Posters of World War Two.* New York: St. Martin's Press, 1973.

Kauffer, E. McKnight. *The Art of the Poster.* London, 1924.

Keay, Carolyn. *American Posters of the Turn of the Century.* London: Academy Editions, 1975.

Kent, Sherman. "War Collection of Yale University Library." *Yale Alumni Magazine*, 22 March 1940.

Lapham, E. F. "The Fourth Liberty Loan: Lend as They Fight." *Fine Arts Journal* 36 (Oct. 1918): 6–13.

Lavine, Harold, and Wechsler, James. *War Propaganda and the United States.* New York: Garland Pub., 1972.

Liberty Loan Committee, 2nd Federal Reserve District. *Report of the Publicity Committee.* New York, 1917.

London. Imperial War Museum. *Second World War Posters by Joseph Darracott and Belinda Loftus.* London, 1972.

Mass Observation. *Government Posters in Wartime.* (Typescript dated 1939, in the Imperial War Museum.)

Meehan Fine Arts. *Fall–Winter 1985–1986 Original WWI & WWII Posters.* New York, [1985]. (Auction catalogue.)

Mercer, Frank Alfred. "Modern Publicity in War." *Modern Publicity* (special issue, [1930?]).

Metzl, Ervine. *The Poster: Its History and Its Art.* New York: Watson-Guptill Publications, 1963.

Mock, James R., and Larson, Cedric. *Words That Won the War: The Story of the Committee on Public Information 1917–1919.* Princeton: Princeton University Press, 1939.

Moses, Montrose J. "Making Posters Fight." *Bookman* 47 (July 1918): 504–12.

N., N. "The War Poster." *The Nation* 107 (14 Sept. 1918): 303–4.

"Navy Posters and Billboards: How American Artists Have Been Helping the Navy." *Sea Power*, August 1917, pp. 12–16.

New Jersey Historical Society. *Collection of World War I Posters.* Chatham, N.J.: Gallery 9 Publications, 1976. (Catalogue of exhibition, sale, and auction at the Museum of the New Jersey Historical Society.)

New York. New School for Social Research. Art Center. *Weimar-Nuernberg-Bonn: An Exhibition of German Posters, May 8 through June 15, 1963, Wollman Hall.* New York, 1963.

New York Public Library. Research Libraries. *Subject Catalog of the World War One Collection.* 4 vols. New York: G. K. Hall, 1961.

"9,000,000 Posters for the Third Liberty Loan." *The Poster* 9 (May 1918): 28.

North Carolina, University of. Ackland Memorial Art Center. *World War One Propaganda Posters: A Selection from the Bowman Gray Collection.* Chapel Hill, 1969. (Catalogue of exhibition, 12 Jan.–23 Feb. 1969.)

Pennell, Joseph. *Liberty-Loan Poster: A Text-Book for Artists and Amateurs, Governments and Teachers and Printers.* Philadelphia: J. B. Lippincott Co., 1918.

Phillips, Duncan. "Art and the War." *American Magazine of Art* 9 (June 1918): 303–9.

The Placard. 1914–1916; resumed publication after the war. (Serial.)

Das Plakat. (Serial.)

Das Plakat: Essays on Propaganda Posters from Das Plakat. N.p., 1914–1919.

Porter, A. Kingsley. "Arms and Art." Art World and Art & Decoration 9 (Oct. 1918): 343–45.

The Poster. (Serial.)

The Poster. War Souvenir Edition. Chicago: Poster Advertising Assoc., 1920.

Poster Photograph Index. Brooklyn, N.Y.: Thomas White.

"Postering the Third Liberty Loan." Literary Digest 56 (23 Mar. 1918): 29–30.

Posters and American War Posters. Published by the Trustees of the Newark Free Public Library, September 1917.

"Posters and Slogans." The Nation 104 (21 June 1917): 728.

Posters of World War I & World War II in the George C. Marshall Research Foundation. Edited by Anthony R. Crawford. Charlottesville: University of Virginia Press, 1979.

"Posters Recently Issued by the National War Garden Commission." The Poster 9 (May 1918): 56.

"Posters to Sweep the United States." Literary Digest 57 (29 June 1918): 30.

"Preparedness Poster by J. Montgomery Flagg." New York Times Magazine, 16 April 1916, sec. 6, p. 5.

Price, Charles Matlack. "The Artists' Call to Colors: The Opportunity of the Poster." Art World and Arts & Decoration 9 (July 1918): 155–57.

Price, Charles Matlack. Poster Design: A Critical Study of the Development of the Poster in Continental Europe, England and America. New, enl. ed. New York: George W. Bricka, 1922.

Price, Charles Matlack, and Brown, Horace. How to Put in Patriotic Posters the Stuff that Makes People Stop—Look—Act! Washington, D.C.: National Committee of Patriotic Societies, 1918.

"Recruiting Posters That Sound a Call to Arms." Cartoons 12 (July 1917): 128–31.

Reuterdahl, Henry. "How the American Artists Are Helping Their Navy." Scientific American 116 (2 June 1917): 552.

Rickards, Maurice. Posters of the First World War. New York: Walker & Co., 1968.

Rickards, Maurice. The Rise and Fall of The Poster. New York: McGraw-Hill Book Co., 1971.

Rowell, Ross E., Captain, U.S.M.C. "Making Marine Corps Posters." Sea Power, July 1917, pp. 22–24.

Rowland, H. L. "Posters Lead in War Loan Campaign." The Poster 8 (Nov. 1917): 36.

Simonson, Lee. "Mobilizing the Billboards." New Republic 13 (10 Nov. 1917): 41–43.

Stanford University. Hoover Institution on War, Revolution, and Peace. War, Revolution, and Peace: Propaganda Posters from the Hoover Institution Archives 1914–1945. [Stanford?, c. 1972.] (Catalogue of exhibition.)

Street, Julian. "Our Fighting Posters." McClure's Magazine 50 (July 1918): 12.

Swann Galleries, Inc. American and European Posters (Auction Sale Number 1186). New York: Swann Galleries, 1980.

Take Up the Sword of Justice: An Exhibition of British World War I Posters from the Special Collections of the Chicago Public Library: Upper Avenue National Bank, John Hancock Center, September 15–October 8, 1976.

"Ten Million Posters for New Loan." The Poster 9 (Oct. 1918): 8.

Theofiles, George. American Posters of World War I. New York: Dafran House Publishers, [c. 1973]. ("A Price and Collector's Guide".)

U.S. Committee on Public Information. Complete Report of the Chairman 1917:1918:1919. Washington, D.C.: U.S. Government Printing Office, 1920.

United States Military Academy. An Era Comes to Life: Eighty-Nine Posters of England, France, Germany and the United States from the Time of the First World War. West Point, N.Y.: United States Military Academy, 1975.

U.S. Navy Department Recruiting Bureau. Recruiting Posters Issued by the Navy since the Declaration of War. [Washington, D.C.?], 1918.

U.S. Public Information Office. Committee on Victory Dinner and Dance of the Division of Pictorial Publication. New York, 1919.

U.S. Shipping Board, Emergency Fleet Corporation, Publications Section. Posters Issued by the United States Shipping Board Emergency Fleet Corporation. Philadelphia, 1918.

"Wake Up, Artists!" Literary Digest 54 (28 April 1917): 1254.

War Information Office. Poster Handbook: A Plan for Displaying Official War Posters. Washington, D.C.: Office of War Information, 1943.

Warren (S. D.) Company. Posters Used by American Industries as War Incentives. Boston: S. D. Warren Company, 1942.

Weitenkampf, Frank. "The War and Lithography." International Studio 65 (Sept. 1918): lxi–lxii.

West Point Museum. Posters for Victory: The American Home Front and World War II: Posters from the West Point Museum: Exhibition 1 August 1978–3 October 1978. West Point, N.Y.: United States Military Academy, 1978.

What Did You Do in the War Daddy? A Visual History of Propaganda Posters. Introduction by Peter Stanley. A selection from the Australian War

Memorial. Melbourne: Oxford University Press, [1983].

Wilson, Louis N. "Posters and Pictures Referring to the European War." *Pedagogical Seminary* 24 (June 1917): 263–71.

Wright, Helen. "Posters and War Work: Library of Congress." *International Studio* 64 (June 1918): cxxi–cxxiv.

Yonkey, Alfred. "Some Recent London Posters." *International Studio* 54 (1915): 281–92.